what this breathing

what this breathing

LAURA ELRICK

THE ELEPHANTS

20 21 22 23 24 5 4 3 2 1

Distributed by Small Press Distribution, Inc.

The Elephants Ltd.
www.theelephants.net

ISBN 978-1-988979-38-0 print

Front cover photo (collaged/adapted):
Fred Kearny via Unsplash

Cover design by Shanna Compton

Interior design by Aimee Harrison

Author Photo by Adriana Varella

Edited by Broc Rossell

CONTENTS

tremblingly my muscled mouth my uncontrolled control

is ownerless, my botanies, when it arcs it

or actual my mouth

starts many-ownered over

at codes exchange my tongue removed removal

dispersing my to smaller dusks, collusions

my mouth's my letter *f* my written lilac

some genetics treated epics trampled virgin

whose purple orientalisms chanting

canoed me drawn to routed aching signs

then my exiled serial commune desperate scolding

then my bio fascist project hungers line

my haymarket my ludlow, my liberia?

whites freedom markets palmerized reforms

its always ever-rising out of changing

tobacco rolled an outsourced data farm

my shaven states my real estate my tactic
calvin-stripped of groin my mouth to gold
my mouth then scaring all the lording johnsons who
dispense their harnessed sense on freakish winds

my mouth my urban planning highway stripping
my mouth my fashion gleaming necks exchanged
my movie shot to pieces ere beginning
by dérive my dada shocked to join

polluted beaker mouth my vat my toxin
by expeditioned substance shook
til nomenclatures whirling sheer my private
my ozone over gaunt and violent grins

my mouth my petalled gape my broken building
my purse my parted works my humming prodder
my starting over in it starter mover
by page my shifting tools our toolings will

what this breathing

DIAGRAM (III)

At a dinner party or forum I rip hair out of my leg with a special machine.
At a panel (part of the symposium) I rip the hair out of my leg with a special machine.
At the seminar I RIP IT OUT
At reception: opening their suits a dress collapsing shoes turn up at odds, strange.
And walking says it would be drinks
And eats the head of their legs with a special machine.
There were ideas and discourses about ideas and gelatinous foods
Fruits ladled inwards, cups of wine.
Irradiating lights zoom downward glistening on their body hair direct them
Out of it.
Ahead: to rip them out to get rid of them to free them with them to be smooth so
Soft is unconscionably mean.
Strangely circling slow motion singular monad and its fifth.
Strangely securing singular monads under the bright light, hanging.
One—it lands between a bookcase and a product stall—woman lost her baby
There's no moral value attached to this.
Enter: intellectual into field.
Trough (nourishment) bookstore circulating the cheese, we hogs.
And who'll be baked for whose mouth stuffed on the walls of what
Apple most beautiful round succulent idolized woman of it
Felt crazy who felt they should leave.
Par tic u lar: as in composed of particles
People an identified instance moving *through* (sans).
This appeared to be happening: ordinary neighborhood, ordinary night.
We had zip codes, IDs, we had credit cards, a quantity of information
A wealth of knowledge it longed to possess.

Felt stimulated. By. For what. Might
Children crawled by on the floor licking their fingers at positives, fingering paints
Appealing up from the floor.
There must've been particles entering our bodies, dangerous poisons
Sick buildings (we are)
From previous eras where different rules applied.
Felt crazy.
Felt the impulse to flee.

Or it was standing before a massive pond, got landscaped.
Up for billowing into bloom from cushions of green feathers—win.
Approach.
Close swimming in dirty particles, impossibly large water pipes into
His slaying grown over analogy.
I was afraid of swimming there afraid, trying to avoid sinking *"to get out of"*
Swimming. In the. Brown. Liner.
The upside, clouds: blue leafy fresh, inverted green.
Began to feel, but in brownwater pipes gurgling slaying ran
If swimming were panicking for having to do so is gender.
Pipes swayed against my legs
Were they my legs?
What. Is. Air—outside.
Light—color, far.
Men walking along an edge, mottled impression.
The of of of what is this strange sense the flight that surrounds the period.
What is this loathsome fear.
The of with him with the everywhere opaque, to repeat
In muddy hair on brown, mirrors the glittering sky. . .
This would adorn a wall.
Then with the length of one of the pipes
Seems sure had vanished or was never there to begin with
I begins to *dance?*
An accident—
Floating in the presence of trees
Toward the murky edge of a body, comma.
The pond as temple, word to their machine.
Rotting in their lovely gowns in dirt and slime.
Slaying in the murky waters.
The fear that captured it pulled it down was
Shoved into the bottom of offering you.
Inhaling it. Drowning in the conscious air.
Enveloping "us"
If this swimming continue forever, a custom.
At any moment you might be piped in.
Some kind of sparkling dome, or

Diagram of the muscles of the face.

Diagram of the muscles of the face.

Small dog watching cat on a table.

Dog approaching another dog with hostile intentions.

Half-bred shepherd dog baring teeth.

Dog—in a humble and affectionate frame of mind.

Diagram of the muscles of the

Cat, savage and prepared to fight.

Cat—in an affectionate frame of mind.

Swan [Diagram]

Swan driving away an intruder.

Hen driving a dog away from her chicks.

Head of a snarling shrew.

Orangutan peaceful, a placid condition.

Orangutan pleased when caressed.

Muscles of marmot.

Diagram of the muscles of the face of the marmot.

Diagram of the muscles of the human child.

Face of female human child.

Photograph of face of human child.

Diagram of human child.

THE MIDNIGHTS OF NOON

She was a notoriously mean woman

excoriating unpredictable prone to rages

known for cutting friendships off abruptly

        to lie is not only to speak some un-truth

I do not tend to remember her as such

though this does not mean I have no memories

of this exhausting side of her

sometimes the lie that is silent is
                                        is to say nothing

only that I was instantly overcome

by the most intense pall of drowsiness

whenever we'd visit I'd fall dead asleep

and be the lie repeatedly, day after day

As if on cue, the sofa in her darkened room

most vivid

memories of her were (because I was awake)

to borrow the sun so long
you burn to ash in its fire

glistening & few. So the. The stories

others tell of my anxiety ring strange to me as dreams

as if viewing a party through a screen door,

and in the freakish light
an atmosphere of all that's left

convinced the figure in outline is one

friend (long dead) only to come to find out

years later it was another. Stomachaches

believe you are at home.

and nightmares, yes? Though the cause was not

but a certain agonizing friction

so thick between her and the others I would sink

if a mind as it stretches
                    toward the smoke says *yeah, yeah,*

Down into the rapturous poisons of

my overgrown sleep and find the thickest

fauna to avoid it. But that is also a story

    do not hurt the interlocutor

and to continue to wander

down a partially obscured path

would be a method of distraction

    by the content of my assertion

Similar in origin to the first. One day

when I was still pretty small, perhaps not long

after some calamitous event in a basement

who might indeed even be lying about lying

    of dog piss and concrete

one of many failed rebellions I was
to spend the night alone with my

you are exposed to none of these perils.

in a house made of heavy gray stone
steep on a hill. She made a special dish
she informed me with mysterious glee

and the instant that I speak

it became one that I would like—as all
children liked it. She beckoned me to follow
I noted her odd joyful shuffle as she rubbed

the difficulty

her hands together and as if on rails, slid
toward the kitchen. There was a marvelous
nook with a built-in semi-circular green bench

while in forthrightly saying I speak

and yellow table around which I slithered

to the far cusp and soon a shallow bowl

was put before me that held the most delicate

difficult because of the illusion that

                                        speech corrects silence

buttery noodles and bits of moist chicken

in a broth where bubbles of grease

floated like stars after rain. After dinner

            passed that something empty fills up

a croaking landing through an octagonal hall

to a bath in a room with green tile then

to be tucked into bed in the "guest room"

doesn't eradicate
                                    silence can never be filled if

                              stared into the darkness.

Strange objects towered and I

wasn't an I, or loomed forward to give me

            if speech itself is a silence

deep inside something anyway

that wasn't mine (though I wouldn't

have structured the thought this way then)

how do you learn to listen to silence

from a previous life many generations

removed The sense I was.

as   eyes adjust to the shadow

    if there is no speech

The wallpaper, dark hole of blue

with scatters of pink and white flowers

on the top half, below which a white half-wall

    to speak is a necessary but impossible task

washed down so the room felt like floating

in the midnight of noon   a large gash

cut diagonally across the side wall

since to speak is to call forth more speech

ominous shadowed crevasse infinitely

deep I remember my father once

narrowing his eyes at it and whispering

        shot through with silence

It needs to be checked the ck thwacking

he meant something I gathered

by a "shitty foundation." I was convinced

                                I think to love

that hundreds of spiders would emerge

from this tectonic but somehow equally subtle

laceration in the wall, this fault-line was a clue

        is a permanent revolution

hidden damage of the house and its danger.

        I refused to fall asleep

instead listening as my

hear the great silences in all speech

moved around in other rooms turning on

and off the lights getting undressed, until at last

I could tell from the silence descending

to still speak

on the still air she slept. Was only then

I got up past the wicker chair and its table

to the glimmering round crystal knob

to be the lie repeatedly, day after day

felt cool in my palm as I turned it.

walked in among the fabrics & silky things

the dress bags and boxes

until the belief that one belongs

that held the hats that no one wore.

The smell was musty but wonderful

like entering the bureau of a queen

wherever one is

what it must be like

so many boxes I didn't have the courage

but neither the desire

because to think   so many

the feeling of it in the joints

treasures I could not possibly

how thick was the dark   her

slippers and bags of gloves

  an ability to present exactly as one is.

In the morning the room chirped in fresh banality

and everything faded back into a regular

day I would later remember

  not guessing about reception

my confusion when I was told that never again

would they take me to be watched by my

  because of the stomachaches

reception does not exist

and to this day I do not know

if I simply   whatever it was

replaced it with this

freakish light

atmosphere of what's left

or whether perhaps the pain didn't arise

from something else, some other stress, were more

vile yet later submerged in a locus

only this embodied sense

of the self, some uncanny children's sense

of the cues of adult bodies that it was

the going   the going there that was

of his being as sending me

to be impossible because they

hated her so much

THINGS TO SMASH

You say: the state, police state, patriarchy and its breaks, broken backs and the tanks, bank windows, white power networks, official and unofficial, pharmaceutical capitalists misogynists and terfs, excessive feelings of fear or vulnerability, refugee camps, excessive feelings of power and self-righteousness, museums, cartesian space linear time, putting the brakes on, no brakes and no breaks

mind-body splitz, weapon hegemony, certain floral things in certain contexts, certain deployments of femininity or masculinity (which ones), landlord, locksmith, certain plaid things in certain contexts, bad vibes, bros, locked condos empty, memories (the material for memories) of unbearable anxiety, amazon warehouses, warehousing amazonia, poetry brokers, World Bank IMF, Exxon flicks

Conoco Phillips Shell, pumpkins, eggs, cop cars, the Harvard school of economics, the Chicago school of economics, glamour, anti-glamour, parochialism, the Calvinist impulses of (even the radical) americans, the nuclear family nuclear power and their offspring prisons, unpaid labor, wage-labor, borders, fences, cages, "that's the breaks" Wall, or the lack of four walls and a roof, too big

to fail, the wanting of privacy, internal boy, chicken farms, slaughter houses, the inability to talk to people unlike you, the inability to talk to people like you, bigotries and objectifications of all kinds, lack of access, exoticizing liberalisms, homophobes, some more corporate windows, data hubs that feed them, did I say white power, agribusiness and its subcontractors, all the insecticides, "pests"

"pesticides," green washing, plastic bags, micro-fiber, beef production, english only, corporate charters, mirrors and computers, anything that breaks, I settler, all that breaking what it already broke, that everything worth nurturing breaks, or nothing breaks and it needs to, now breaking all around us since the atom, and that seconds break, that even a nano-second breaks, that 'break' breaks

KINDLING

If the provoking cop is also a smasher.

Blue object blocks the release.

Toxicity associated with the color blue.

She touched the center of another's palm

And bowed her head

And posted it.

If blue shards pulse from a torso.

The provoking cop is also a smasher.

Tranquility or toxicity, is the color blue?

Whose insights play with the smasher.

(If the provoking cop is also a smasher).

Things to smash: you say the state.

Anything that breaks.

REVOKED

Everything breaks.

The detox is already beginning.

You move the object aside.

Shards of insight escape.

You you

You

Blue object.

Becoming a what.

To goad, spur, prod, rouse.

To stir, excite, inflame, to spark.

The trigger—pull it?

Provoke the cop. Is a warning.

A provoking cop in a body shield.

That which protects but encloses.

Suffocating.

Move it aside

And the shards burst out.

Interiority

That really sickens provoking cops.

You are no longer never whole.

Pro- forth

-Vocare to call

Provocare

The shard is that which ruptures continuity.

Tranquility is the blue that is toxic.

To the one that it heals?

That healing is toxic, that it makes you sick.

Blue shards pulse from her eyes to her torso.

Her is a time and a place.

Exploding shards are what is left, an H

That loses its ladder.

And e with no eye.

An r with no leg.

The antidote itself is toxic.

We blast her out of the continuum.

The powerful but sickening shard.

Blocked but powered by blue objects.

That is, by provoking cops.

But if the provoking cop is also a smasher.

The provoking cop is also a smasher.

The affinity structure's name of the father.

Exploding out of her chest.

REVS MASHEEN

In the cave-hole the sun was shining. People darted about making stew. Some were singing, some pounded spoons on what had been abducted from industry's garbage bin, while the students of technology looked on, grimacing. They tried to instruct us with the authority of editors, whose eagle-eyed corrections tend to come in a list:

1) We're not looking on, we're looking forward to looking back!
2) You can do that [~~til death~~] too.
3) Go quickly, young man.

But upon the completion of the reading of the corrections, noticing the carnival of indifference that had begun to swing from the rafters, and haughtily refusing the juice of the pears on their chins, the editors began to flail as they gesticulated the time:
it's 3:27! it's. . .
3:28!
. . .it's 3:29!

Bird tossed her pot, picked up her sling shot and aimed.

"Time-Running-Out" dove under the bar to drink scotch, "No-Place-But-Here" smashed up a number of stools, "Let-Me-Remember-My-Youth" placed fatally their vitals between a mob and the juke-box.

Amidst all the uproar, it was Luminousness killed the clock quite demurely: we got me to shoot it.

crack shatter a blurry droove
dive bungles a bloody nose
and swinging
strode out in a clowde of duste

Then the metal beneath me moves, and I'm suddenly being buzzed toward the tube.

Panic wells up and inexplicably the skin above my lip begins to itch. Unbearable breathing out, I mean to blow on it, to scratch it with air from my lungs. But the itch gets worse, as if a single agitated hair is dangling over the skin.

"Wait" I say in a moment of desperation. And the table on which I am lying, crisp white sheets wrapped tightly around the body and arms making of me a kind of sterilized sausage, comes to a mechanical halt.

I can't turn my head far enough to see the stern-looking technician, but I hear his voice beaming in from across the glass partition. "Is there a problem— ?"

Um. I.

Need to scratch my nose.

Thungson, Swan (according to the name badge studied earlier, as if to glean my fortune there) waits, if not patiently then silently. (Can feel him watching through the observation window). Enters and stuffs the sheets tightly under my arms. I hear the metal door slam, but forget I'm mic'd:

"Butt wad" I mutter, and he stops me again, *Problem?*

I/psychologist purses her lips, and it is then at that moment that "I see."

The architect has placed a skylight above the patient.

In the basement of an institution, the heavy machinery: branches and leaves above.

Arc and glint.

I had come here with the desperate though somewhat skeptical hope of being healed. This was the law of discourse: I had to comply. Trays and gowns, stainless steel—such were the necessary if-then logics, logics. What was off—to the side? Innocuous-looking foyers that suggested restrooms or stairwells but were clearly marked in an officially appropriate font: MASOCHISTIC DAYDREAMS CLINIC, and CENTER FOR THE STUDY OF SELF-PROTECTIVE PAIN MECHANISMS—SOCIAL UNIT.

These clinical offices, these vestibules of monetized care—sometimes they were entirely self-contained worlds, replete with the ambient strain of their respective disorders, fetishizing the natural discomfort of the place by making it appear fashionable, with an atmosphere of mist, for example, or a collection of poisonous blue frogs synthing across the moss-covered concrete.

It was here in one corner by the spider terrarium that I found her whom I loved, leaning against a shadow.

She was a breakdown of character, a device I had grown accustomed to calling my "sister." We were exquisitely porous, each of her spaces fabricated me with the force of the cinema (inside her). Social punctuation was lifting our heads back in transit, between orffices, up toward the light blue hole. A bird soaring across that framed space, utter silence. That bird was, I mean, my sister. Now believed to be heading in the direction of Aldebaran located in the Taurus constellation. Though she has yet to pass the heliopause and Oort's cloud we now know her progress to be the negative matter through which all shadows that are forms fall.

We are the discoverers of worlds: new, and yet known.

At first it would seem that the limits of the one reside in a wall that is the other's mask. But this wall entombs us in a matrixial tactilic ambience, in a light-colored plastic, in a militarized womb.

Which comes first in the wounding of a wor(l)d, the prick or the knead, the wall or the tube. The body is not on one side of it, it is *in* it. Track-lights line the roof of the thing, which is so close to the face one can't focus. How to ob-serve that which has covered the verry eyye?

Like being all alone in a personal body-sized jet you're forced to lie down in, a tobogganed device for steering: and that's a body? *Like* this (but not *being* it) you are totally looking out of its windows while rain pelts against them, streams off. You're "inside," teeming like rain. Because inside expands, swells to fill this enclosure, it is no longer your skin but a surface farther away, a barrier that would not even be noticeable if it were not keeping you in (or out), something wet (dry on the inside) or dry (wet on the inside) battering insidiously and pointlessly against a pane.

In the tube, magnets manipulate a motor and you hear metallic jerks and grinds, patterns you associate with music. They tap and jolt, tear the silence with an oppressively regular but varying sound, like serial monogamy. Sudden alterations make an illusion of chance, a hypnosis of gears bangs some invisible inner track that shifts with the precision of an instrument. It's perfectly objective. Delusional.

FLAURA & FAUNA

1,
—lit—

Once there
        could have been

Her curves there were dreams though
I had acted institutions defined to her delights

I smelled her scent everywhere
I shirked owed and esteemed
But the grids became proofs

Of sequestered bluffs—her carefully monitored 'health'

Doors   through wrapping one's acting

The gendered mind's
androgynous body

Combining is a dream

Not as a film squanders peasants did I love him
nor to the firms' calibrations

But no rubric resists
The object's procedure

If all might be laid bare

what should be read, dear

should be read dear

2.

So that's what entails
so managed exclusion

That's not corruption
the ulcerous groom

Your address
            overshot
a failed fairness

But I didn't mean but I
well I knew

So right
            he's nothing
he profits from

Woman?

We tap our clits with gavels
even the pastured she-goats

skipping past (what past) condones

So it's said no paper no voice
so collects its poor ripostes

so old men sneer and
women recoil so that's what

What did they expect
drear
dear

And medicine, so, and prescription

noxious or sweet—the same

So uproot as that's an organic

so unplug as
that's no reply

Cared for, torn
so left of indecision

human and forlorn
a centrist to delusion

You, audience, you my friends
or
you, audience, who do not yet live
or
you, audience, adamantly drawn

You, audience yclept
when the hail storm

Is hewn to elegant stasis

Do soothe some

But this quiet's
a tirade

a blue oppression

"my curved points
slope"

3,
—crowd—

That you've decided to call
now, as the blinking has stopped

And given all devices
what's to be used?

Up away into thin air comes back
as where we move

crossing one another on the sidewalk

What stopped you—clasped waiting
in crisis, patient, fill

while the era's locked display is
corporatizing glances

and what woes in what private gauze
tick there in head in fibers what

I thought you were asking

4,

—isle—

May you sleep on the bosom

of your tender companion

5,
—ject—

“Hey you”

protestant will

What clings
single body

as if the aged stranger
is
waltzing waltzing

Forced mourning

is morning
applauding a monitor

bravo crowds must
decrepit as the flag

Happily deaf—exact

is back

The plot extant
asa stream that skriketh still

and moving forward
is a blue boon
in his wet dream

Let me be desired

let me be the one
gracefull
y as

that purple plumbed
thumb

Said he

architecturally

6,

"So what I suggest is that you. . ."
amid pages leafing

the stick-shift

memory:

Cast it out catholic

as an urban trinity
privation
hives &
honey
combs

(absent riposte)

don't—respond

I, a
strange way of doing
my necktie

ever seen a marionette
who can run like mine?

(visualize fonts

scroll over the flats
owning)

A flat thing

today'd me to flat things
on the way

there were cameras

(The hot day
a hot scent
rising up from her lap)

parting the legs just slightly
atmospheres the train

'Anything'
could happen
piloted by ledgers

bird-free

Not particularly
there
were we

me and my lap

at the luncheon

"do you?"

lemons

"My flora"
"My paper-clipped selections"

IT IS A VIOLENT ROTATING COLUMN OF AIR

On a bench in front of a café, little general store, bakeshop, country kitchen. Narrow median cutting the street. Row of trees planted on a ridge between ranges. Swirling ones loose at their roots.

This precarious shaking between parallel earths, a diaphanous sky what is "solid."

Someone says look at those trees they don't look right.

You stand up—run for the delicate café door. Grasp the effete knob. Down to a cellar, *the* cellar you think, a vast dim room of boilers painted dull green, its sub-marine sea of red gauges blinking. You blink too.

The gauges spin red light over the zone, then a waft of damp concrete and you begin to smell it, utterly human.

You will come across a small, lost girl who wants to hide a letter from her mother. Do you tell her you will help her, but not in the machinery? Not in the machinery.

If you press the knobs and the chemicals threaten, then. . . See? You tell her. What good is a letter to anyone. But oh, alright, you can put it with the thing in this high cabinet.

Just go on and try to take another one's girl-child's letter. But not in this tornado! Not in the tornado. Cubby holes fill with conservative families, do you offend them. What is it.

THEY MADE THE CALL AND I WENT

The street the field the highway
All of it without any people
Highway to nowhere
Electrical wires
On posts the lights still on

At first in the houses
But then they turned those off
We'd be driving around
And a wild boar would jump out
The school building

At us or else a rabbit
Everywhere animals
Instead of people
The posters still hanging our goal
Is the happiness of mankind
With liberty and justice for be all

You can be we ask
Each other is this what our life
Is like? The first time we saw it
Smack to the head what
Is born in disaster

But we shoot for science too
One time we shot two rabbits

Two foxes two wild goats
They're all sick but we

Tenderize them
At first we were afraid

But now we're used to it
You have to eat something we

Can't all move to the moon

We met soldiers there
They had masks gloves
Armored personnel carriers
And we're in shirts
Handkerchiefs over our noses

I got together two brigades
Each had a veterinarian
And someone from the epidemic

Center we also had a tractor
A scooper and a dump truck
It's too bad they didn't give us any
Protection didn't think about
Cheap cotton, like a cook's

We rode around that place for months
Half the towns in our region
Evacuated dozens of them
The first time we came the dogs

Were running near the houses
Waiting for the people
To come back they were happy
To see us they ran toward our voices

We shot them shot them
In the houses in barns in the yards
We'd drag them out into the street
Onto the dump truck

It wasn't very nice they couldn't
Understand *Why we are killing*
Them it was easy
They were household pets
They ran toward our voices

They're all sick but we still
Tenderize them and eat
Show the dosimeter
Again this is meat

Doesn't taste like what
You have to eat something
From a collapsing bridge
It will be seeds

That will bring them down
Lodged in the seams or rusting
Saw trees into pieces
Pack them in cellophane and

Throw them into graves
Birds evaporate the worms
Disappear the lilacs don't smell
The trees are scared too

But they're quiet
We go to the store
And we take some milk
It isn't from an animal

It's from nuts the nuts
Sucked the last water
From the dwindling aquifer
It suffered

Low rainfall farm runoff
The cow on the box
Etc. and someone says
That's why I used to drink rice

It's a picture of health really
Really healthy like and

The cow grassfed and penned
Is this what a life is like

You can't buy your way out
We can't all move to the moon
Suckling the teats of the cow
That jumped over

Half the towns
Could not sleep at night
At first we were afraid
Of animals instead of people

They ran toward our voices
At first we were afraid
Handkerchiefs over our noses
You have to
Eat something: shame
Shoot them
They didn't send us any
Protection didn't think about
The people made the call
And I went

NORMAL STATES

You've got to get up hold on here
and here the bright postcolonial sun
melting the feverish object for a haze

sentimentalizing film
in the image of a history that only read
like a picture, this shot toward the sun

woozy angle the anti-souvenir
of a host for colonies clung
what are you doing there but running

unawares but sickened to the heart of it
personal torments a puppet for the state
around his waist days lost on a mattress

back of the motor bike your arms
on a floor, hobbling down a hall
you could keep nothing down, nothing in

by the time the boy came, so lithe
another day the doctor said
another day just one and you might not have

by the time the boy came, so lithe
another day left to shield your eyes
another day the doctor said

just one and you might not have even
one piece of dry baguette the colonial host
would be to vomit but to eat

the little sandwiches with the soft cheese
with the chilis and cilantro delicious
in the street it came on so fast

you did it in the gutter by a hip café
days weeks a month
your limp body and helped you to the cot

from the wavering zones, the spots
of sun-drenched haze
and when at last you found a telephone

they had no sense of where you were
or how anyone lived the hospitals
had no soap it was difficult to go

find a place to sit and order something
small, a tea perhaps or water, to count
the money that a normal state takes

think do not pass the military trucks
nothing down nothing in, their white high
roll bars & lights like a pickup built for hunting

like a pick-up built for hunting why you
were there, a backwash of the schools, what you
already knew, chest of tortured skulls

windowless room the partially exhumed
lavender dress, child-sized pocket, it was
just there, decades later, the metallic pills

couldn't keep them down, nothing in, skin
you weren't, you weren't anything yet
but a privilege of leaving oh god she said

less spoken than exhaled we thought
you were dead and you were dead
for having been thought so and it was

the kind of dying that happens everywhere
in this state inside the state of every state
you swallow because you want

yes want to live and
that is the start of complicity that
only a blush burns and then obedience

tinged with a burgeoning else
an anxiety in the host you know you are
and will learn you want to, no, must kill

SLURRY PUMP

To find it depressing, to wade barefoot through sludge, toward the hull of a rusting ship rent in half (it could have been a Gordon Matta-Clark) except you live there, actually.

After scooping the sludge into buckets and lugging them the half mile or so up the beach, you come back to the wall as it collapses, sending clouds of red dust up over the ledge of your hiding place, where you squat.

To think that all those lessons (guppy, minnow, porpoise, shark) could have prepared you for this type of breathing. A poem for the future then.

To recover gas from the coal beds and to prevent the escape of fugitive gas. It is, in a way, a slurry pumped to the surface.

POST-INDUSTRIAL ROAM

[\

Adulation

stepping into the worlds soft breezes

the curiously undivided yet

or strolls
unusually slowly less to locate

it.

What's recaptured

climbing shivers not
in sectioned parts

but the ghosted factory's
carts. . .

rusting still

Who's out walking
the warehouse ruins.

That bricks denude
to walkway's hang

the echoing taps

busily empty

To turn
forward coming back has

(since then)

broke:

If those jagged games boys armed
winnowing seeds to industry

shattered windows

abandon sprouts through breaking
what barriers now.

Workers
ghostily working

tromping chemicals strange caresses

dirt there now holds it)

[\

Had I wondered before
had I made the wrong decision

had executive gamed
deform by all accounts

Spied and spised
that which it kindled

had time been spent.

Did the savage awake
to harken abductions.

Did the alcoholic sweats produce delight.

I watched another watching
another watching when I looked

mooded wildness
blisters in a brooding ocean

a local anesthesia

plotted more malls.

Does the bandwidth
destroy particulars?

A course in resignation
protected them from misery

disrupted the fountains of

temps perdu. . .

Where to keep
bad things hidden—it was *trash*

can't be stealing

Had reciprocity   had puncture

had children

(that's ten squared
plus square root of twenty

over three)

Had night as day

subdivided   duplication)

[\

Touchless burns
I make it my own brow

what isn't subject.

This site's
non-load-bearing walls

They keep in
different parts.

More cell division

digits appear

with the sun—truck routes

Having made it
one began to feel trapped there.

There were paper birds
large as Volvos
soaring gusts

they collapsed
in deep quiet drapes
of domestic
snow

What coats the mess—disdain?

Democratic passions
erupt far away

ashes bury the incorporated person.

A good story is
a failure

means more work to do. . .

I spent my ambition there

idle as in
rots on the docks.

Love examine
the amendment

does it gape or stitch
to hole me)

[\

What duplicates for the judge
what dockets amass

In crepuscular data
heedless to confusion

The house shot through

Form B253691-9 can't prove it

Though your limb's blown out
the back of your jeans
and you limp

surge

Not really a place

An inventory skills its
abilities deploy them

co-produced by

non-looks over
state your name for the record

It must be
judicial Taylorism

Well, she can't read replies
well at least not—well the state claims

Code Z7422-2

No family? Injured? Can't make the rent?

[\

The garden. . .plot.

Rifles through pages
before the block party

if there is one.

Abrogates domestic formula
for daft life.

Paralyzed age
outlined to make it look deeper.

The sky—virtually flat
darts over several stories

smart. . .what. . .?

Yarn-and-finger stars, flight path whatever
just tell me how much I owes.

Pleasant
has all you need in a personality

lives right here with my
writerly American cousin

antibiotically smiling.

War Planes and the Pedicurists
(a mystification)

WarPlanes: *(into a mic)*

Regime change, counting on defections!
Are you from 'Seoul'?

Pedicurists: *(laughing furiously)*

Sol de Oaxaca—
Look at these ladies' feet!

Eyes puncture

space of the sidewalk

prospective desires
chart sideways off a curb)

[\

Indelible odor

x-perambulator
rickety immanence.

What made these channels
charnels to wade through read into

"engagements" motorists deploy

(extolls appeals to order)
(eyelid muscle spasms)

He's parceled
rejuvenation

forced floating on pockets of air.

I walked there mom

I felt my toes lifted right
up over my head

an asshole's target

for a bluebird.

The danger was there
but transcribed.

Events
a nacreous backdrop ignores

presses
their quantum horror.

My shiny red toe eye
loves you so

7mm left of your latch
hook neck

rubber feeling.

Two four six eight
stair climbing
pennies plus accumulated
four three inch
books

Tug me those flower scents off the
top rack could you)

[\

In greenish corridors
we will lick you like linoleum

but we won't bear you
any more children

(spaces talk

but maybe not to you).
The floor below is weeping,

stooping
knuckles tell it

no violent now.

We were hydrochemically anywhere
knowing a war was coming

preparation daily in the questions

nocturnal crops—people
yet to glean.

You don't feel your body
fall away.

Caught in a circular rising

taut from lifting

what ignores.

Shouldered graceful as water

what rewards)

[\

Not Mrs. Pastry Inc.
may-we-hide-under-yr-skirts

long waiting steams
to hold back future sleep

In the cryogenic pink glow
of the uterine bayou.

I mean
inner
minus the christian billboards
micro bulbs

Watts link me to ice shelves
fallen in the sea.

Know it—
there is no collective address.

Only acts of god
acts of man or
acts of revolution
it's just

Not in the contract

Actual Evaporation.

The balls of her feet
in plate glass
floating)

IF I SPEAK

If I speak in dashes—in ellipses, is the silence louder?
Whose magnificent ears float beneath an eyeball
and the moon. The Great Dying will nevertheless be lived through
An intersubjective space.
We might not have the language to mark
the archive—but of rocks
is what the theme of such a night was.
What kind of art should be made for it?
If there will have been a human story
but not the one we tell ourselves.

LIFE IN THE VASE

In the mirror world, she has cut off her arm at the elbow, whereas the daytime of the real demands an aloof feminine poise (though everything depends on which industry). To save the identity essence at its core even the mutilated dream limb can be turned into a vase when positioned correctly. I feel like a new woman. I feel like a _____. Correct is rigorous but upside down. What cannot *ever* be recognized has four arms, three that are attached. It can stick their thumb in the flesh of the fourth to open it, like an orange.

RAGE AND POPPIES

She is there, split into four she's, a single she most legible, not brighter than the rest.

Together they wait in line for something everyone needs, hence their patience in waiting. They do not believe their need for the thing is more than the need of any of the others. Even the poppy waits.

When I compare her to a flower, I wade into the human sea without any real ability to resist the undertow of discursivity. My heart "leaps" when I see her.

I drag my women behind me to pass through the grove of she's she has become.

It is a gauntlet that we, my women and I, must pass through again and again, approaching a necessity that is its end but that always seems to recede.

This receding is a failure that gives and gives.

The wrinkles faintly inscribed beneath the lover's eyes prove it.

Sometimes she or one of the four she's she has split into dies, and four more sprout in the dead one's place, making seven.

Of the seven she's she has become, one is killed by snipers, one dies in police custody under suspicious circumstances, one is shot by an unnamed employee of a federal agency, one dies in childbirth, one drowns in the aftermath of a hurricane, one withers away in a misery of bad choices in love.

All of these deaths are social deaths. None are distributed evenly on the bodies in the realm.

Yet from each death, four more sprout and now there are twenty-eight.

Of the twenty-eight she's we move among, now a crowd, toward what is always receding, pulling our selves behind us, gently, like a horse, two fingers in my mouths, most will remain disinterested when I split into four she's and she splits into four she's, and the twenty-eight become thirty-six.

And of the thirty-six she's waiting in line for something that everyone needs, hence their patience in waiting, roughly half come to learn selves-devotion.

In learning this they learn devotion for another, for many others, they grow new eyes new arms new organs to go fight to go fugitive to go fuck to heal the scarred poppies in the heart.

The other half do what they can to drown the wounds, or to flaunt them, which is the same thing, a perpetuation of their suffering.

Often half of one's she's devote, half suffer, and no one becomes the four-fourths that are one.

In a crowd like this, when I compare her to a flower, I wade into a human sea without any real ability to resist the undertow of discursivity. My heart "leaps."

The math explodes, the math fragments, the math blooms.

The maths scatter like dust, like pollen.

THE GROVE

The lovers take turns hoisting each other above their shoulders in the shadowed light.

With preternatural skill, they unhook their scapulae from the conceptual scapulae, their pelvises from the conceptual pelvis, their throats from the conceptual throat.

Then they return all the concepts to the flesh but in a disparate order.

It begins like this. Until exhausted, they board the trains with their thigh is a belly, the heart in a throat.

Colors seep through their chests onto the street, social and anonymous, tendering the air around them into scarlets, tangerines, a pale, fresh pink.

Sometimes they die, or are killed by the state.

Sometimes they survive, but their hearts leak the aftermaths in gray.

Occasionally what brushes a chest or a shoulder surprising, a purified green glows through.

When the trains once again return them to the grove their manliness quivers toward energy, buoyed by the strength of their womanly voices, which are courageous and bell-like.

Her hands are large and the muscled ropes of her arms reach toward the dark sky, to draw down, slowly, expertly, what they are beginning to become.

Leopards or bats.

No one will know us except our future lovers calling us through the portals, mutable and redressed.

To approach the overgrown fence through an undulating shadow of leaves that darkens and descends to protect them from the lamps.

The fence is cast iron around a plot of empty grass, the nothing of property they despise but were born in.

Often they talk of scaling the fence.

But the inside, who really wants it, until their cocks melt or their pussies get wet for her hands, which will die.

(Light is a ploy, we evade its sea of police, darting away from our labels).

Where's my hat, one murmurs, arching up over the architectural horizon. And another one touches the small of her back to call it back down to the park bench.

Sleep arrives later in a room somehow, for some of them, who are lucky.

Then a crack of light, industrial chatter, steel cuts through time.

(Now is another now, always here in us, hearing us).

In its true hallucination, police strobes, a pickup truck, shouts, threat of violence, a mob of whites masquerade as neutral.

To cross this river, you must cross the digitized event stream, then cross back.

Now lie on your back, the lover murmurs.

The sternum blooms toward hands that are distant, on the other side of the river but coeval, somehow still holding the hips from behind.

To de-member the mob that mutilated the bodies they were once, before they found their new bodies.

Unstoppable, uneradicable, unending.

Pantherlike, batlike.

They drop down again.

METHANE SEA

Immersed in it off the early morning beach. No, immerse is inaccurate—they float, eye-burn in salt and sun. Let a whoop when a wave lifts up, the water unfurls its stage.

Companions heart housed off camera, beyond the secure perimeter, taken by waves and dragged under, the video clip on repeat.

What does not make loving for the world-at-large a momentary suspension, an expanse, the sea itself.

Deposited in shallow water, pile of upturned sand, some skin left, slack momentum, no shells.

And with legs we're back to the present: two scientists appear under a parachute. The parachute buoys a research laboratory under which enormous apparati perch like spiders one reckons with in knobs, attention relaxed, dialed-in, analytic.

The other one works a station on the busier side, preparing a platform for the arrival of data, under which and through all must walk.

No, works is inaccurate. They float on a foot-mind, an absence under the laboratories.

Slowly come back to waterless muscle, and that's task.

Is it "air" that they study? Do they love what they do?

ACKNOWLEDGMENTS

The last section of "Diagram (III)" employs figure captions from Charles Darwin's *The Expression of the Emotions in Man and Animals;* the poem is also inspired by the late work of Eva Hesse. Many of the lines in "They Made The Call and I Went" are taken from *Voices from Chernobyl: The Oral History of a Nuclear Disaster* by Svetlana Alexievich, Trans. Keith Gessen. "The Midnights of Noon" is in conversation with Foucault's lectures collected in *Fearless Speech* (Ed. Joseph Pearson), and it recontextualizes some of the sentences from that book. Many thanks to Francie Shaw for the invitation to respond to some of the collages in her *Rex Works* series: "Life in the Vase" and "If I Speak" emerged from that collaboration.

Versions of some of these poems first appeared in the journals *Cannot Exist, Try, Filling Station, President's Choice, Public Access, Boog City, The Felt* and *Magazine Cy Press*; thanks to the editors. Thanks also to Michael Cross and Rich Owens for printing a beautiful broadside of an early version of "Methane Sea."

The poems in this book were drafted and reworked slowly but consistently over a very large number of years, almost a decade and a half. I could not have completed the work without the presence of many brilliant friends, colleagues, healers, loves, and I am deeply grateful for the support, large and small, offered at key moments over the years. Thank you especially to Emily Beall, Tracy Grinnell, Rachel Zolf, Ellery Washington, Rodrigo Toscano, Clint Burnham, Christian Hawkey, Christine Hume, Lee Katz Maxwell, Zahra Patterson, Mirene Arsanios, Terrie Mystique, Rijard Bergeron, and John Elrick—each of you made it feel more possible to write this book (and myself) into existence. Thank you also to my love, Adriana Varella, for bringing such expansiveness, creativity, and joy to life always, and for believing in my work. Thank you especially and profoundly to Broc Rossell for the extraordinary editorial suggestions, to Jordan Scott for talking so generously with me about early drafts of the manuscript, and to The Elephants for ushering this book into the world.

LAURA ELRICK is a poet, essayist, educator, and performance writer based in Brooklyn, NY. Previous works include *Propagation* (Kenning Editions, 2012), *Fantasies in Permeable Structures* (Factory School, 2005), and *Skincerity* (Krupskaya Books, 2003), as well as the trans-media performances *Stalk* (2008) and *Blocks Away* (2010). Her work has appeared in the anthologies *Viz. Interarts: Interventions*, and *The Eco Language Reader*, as well as in numerous journals including *BOMB*, *Mandorla*, *The Brooklyn Rail*, *XCP: Cross-Cultural Poetics*, LINE, and *Aufgabe*. She is Associate Professor of Writing at Pratt Institute.